LEADING ADVISOR

VOL. 2

SPOTLIGHTS ON REMARKABLE FINANCIAL PROFESSIONALS AND ADVISORS

LEADING ADVISOR

VOL. 2

SPOTLIGHTS ON REMARKABLE FINANCIAL PROFESSIONALS AND ADVISORS

LEADING FINANCIAL PROFESSIONALS AND ADVISORS

FEATURING:

Jonathan Taylor

Gregory Kojak

Eric A. Dupré

Adam D. Koos

Jacob Chrysler

Michael Chrisler

Shanna Tingom

Gabrielle Kelly

Michael P. Nelan

Brock Brenneman

Remarkable Press™

Royalties from the retail sales of **“LEADING ADVISOR Vol. 2: SPOTLIGHTS ON REMARKABLE FINANCIAL PROFESSIONALS AND ADVISORS”** are donated to the Global Autism Project:

AUTISM KNOWS NO BORDERS;
FORTUNATELY NEITHER DO WE.®

The Global Autism Project 501(C)3 is a nonprofit organization that provides training to local individuals in evidence-based practice for individuals with autism. The Global Autism Project believes that every child has the ability to learn, and their potential should not be limited by geographical bounds. The Global Autism Project seeks to eliminate the disparity in service provision seen around the world by providing high-quality training to individuals providing services in their local community. This training is made sustainable through regular training trips and contiguous remote training. You can learn more about the Global Autism Project and make direct donations by visiting **GlobalAutismProject.org.**

Leading Advisor Vol. 2/ Mark Imperial —1st ed.

Managing Editor/ Shannon Buritz

ISBN: 978-1-954757-14-1

CONTENTS

A NOTE TO THE READER

Thank you for obtaining your copy of "LEADING ADVISOR Vol. 2: Spotlights on Remarkable Financial Professionals and Advisors." This book was originally created as a series of live interviews; that's why it reads like a series of conversations, rather than a traditional book that talks at you.

My team and I have personally invited these professionals to share their knowledge because they have demonstrated that they are true advocates for the success of their clients and have shown their great ability to educate the public on the topic of Financial Planning.

I wanted you to feel as though the participants and I are talking with you, much like a close friend or relative, and felt that creating the material this way would make it easier for you to grasp the topics and put them to use quickly, rather than wading through hundreds of pages.

So relax, grab a pen and paper, take notes, and get ready to learn some fascinating insights from our Leading Advisors.

Warmest regards,

Mark Imperial
Publisher, Author, and Radio Personality

INTRODUCTION

"LEADING ADVISOR Vol. 2: Spotlights on Remarkable Financial Professionals and Advisors" is a collaborative book series featuring leading professionals from across the country.

Remarkable Press™ would like to extend a heartfelt thank you to all participants who took the time to submit their chapter and offer their support in becoming ambassadors for this project.

100% of the royalties from this book's retail sales will be donated to the Global Autism Project. Should you want to make a direct donation, visit their website at GlobalAutismProject.org

JONATHAN TAYLOR

JONATHAN TAYLOR

Conversation with Jonathan Taylor

Jonathan, you are a Financial Advisor with Northwestern Mutual based in New York City. Tell us about your work and the people you help.

Jonathan Taylor: First and foremost, I love to help people who want to be helped. I can lead a horse to water, but I can't necessarily make it drink. When I have clients who want to work on their financial planning, it is always my goal to help them however I can – that's what I'm passionate about.

A little bit about me, I'm an engineer by trade. In the financial advising world, I'm what they call a "career changer." I started as an engineer from the Rochester Institute of Technology in upstate New York. That is why I love working with mathematicians, engineers, and scientists as clients because they like to know how all of the nickels and dimes work. Also, I am very fortunate in my career to be able to spend 20 percent of my practice's time working with underserved communities. I try to help close the gap in regards to providing access to financial planning throughout their lifetime.

How has the recent pandemic impacted the financial services industry?

Jonathan Taylor: The most important thing I've seen is people reviewing their financial plans more than ever before. Also, younger generations are now looking at their financial planning. The 2008 "once in a lifetime" financial crisis is now happening for a second time, so people realize they need to be way ahead of the curve to access information and technology to prepare for the next potential crisis. I often receive questions about reducing credit card debt that people have accrued throughout the pandemic and how to shore up emergency funds.

Are there common myths and misconceptions about financial planning?

Jonathan Taylor: Unfortunately, one of the biggest issues is there are so many resources available today. You could read 100 different books and get 100 different answers on how to do your financial planning. You should look for a financial planner from a reputable company with a respected brand name behind it. Also, consider the acumen of the planner with regards to designations, titles, and accomplishments. No matter what you do, you're going to read advice from all over the place, right? Comparatively, you could be one of the few lucky individuals who happen to be at the right place at the right time, but we know that is few and far between, and the minority, not the majority. That mindset is not going to be a way to shore up financial security, which of course, is the actual result and goal of financial planning. Whichever company you choose to work with, and whichever information you choose to read, make sure it is reputable, not a random thread in social media.

What mistakes do you help your clients avoid?

Jonathan Taylor: Many young people diversify their asset classes across multiple financial institutions. They'll have a savings account here, a checking account there, another savings account over here. Consolidating your assets with one financial institution can help lower your fees and rates. People tend to try to separate their money because they are afraid an institution could have solvency problems. They want to have a safety net, so to speak. But if they are banking below the $250,000 FDIC insured amount, which is actually a government-sponsored program, then there's a guardrail.

The other mistake I see people making is trying to accrue debt to increase their credit score, thinking that is the best way to keep their credit up. I want to make sure my clients have access to their credit when they need it in this day and age. I help educate them on the ideal ways to secure their credit score.

Jonathan, what inspired you to get started in the financial services field?

Jonathan Taylor: I've been an entrepreneur since I was a child. I incorporated my first company in the state of New York at the age of seven years old. I was fixing computers for family and friends, and my mother helped me incorporate my computer repair company. My mother, an amazing woman, won Jimmy Carter's Business Woman of the Year Award in 1977. She went down to the White House and received a commendation. Both sides of my family have always had an entrepreneurial spirit, as my father's family started their business in 1934, surviving for 82 years in America. Unfortunately, it sold in 2016. The way my firm's practices are set up, I still get to be an entrepreneur. I love leading my practice and having the backing of Northwestern Mutual. Being able to remain a self-starter in a meritocracy, give back to my community, and help people, has been really powerful for me.

How can people find you, connect with you, and learn more?

Jonathan Taylor: My office's number is 212-812-0519, but I always carry my cell phone, and the number is 347-723-7428. I work off my cell phone because, in the financial space, you don't want to hear from your advisor, "Hey, I'm out of the office right now." You can also email me at jon.e.taylor@nm.com. My website is www.jonetaylor.nm.com. A simple Google search of Jonathan Taylor at Northwestern Mutual will lead you to me as well.

Northwestern Mutual is the marketing name for The Northwestern Mutual Life Insurance Company (NM) (life and disability Insurance, annuities, and life insurance with long-term care benefits) and its subsidiaries, including Northwestern Long Term Care Insurance Company (NLTC) (long-term care insurance), **Northwestern Mutual Investment Services, LLC (NMIS)** (investment brokerage services), a registered investment adviser, broker-dealer, and member of FINRA and SIPC, and Northwestern Mutual Wealth Management Company® (NMWMC) (investment advisory and trust services), a federal savings bank. NM and its subsidiaries are in Milwaukee, WI.

Jonathan Evan Taylor is an Insurance Agent of NM and NLTC. Investment brokerage services provided as a Registered Representative of **NMIS**. Investment advisory services provided as an Advisor of NMWMC.

JONATHAN TAYLOR

Financial Advisor

Northwestern Mutual

As an engineer in college, Jon was trained that every problem has a solution. As a fourth-generation businessman from an entrepreneurial family, he was taught that the true essence of work is to do a good and fair job for clients. With these lessons in mind, he succeeded by following his family's motto: "Whatever it takes!"

As President of his family's wholesale hardware business, he modernized, grew, and when it was time, sold it to a public company. After ensuring a smooth transition, he took some time to consider his next career move. He realized how much he could contribute to helping people solve everyday problems and is now proud to be part of the world's strongest financial services firm. He strengthens his clients by supporting them, planning for them, and helping them identify and reach their financial goals via customized solutions. From this level of personalization, each client becomes an important member of his family.

He is the Northwestern Mutual NYC-Midtown Office's Pacesetter 40 & Pacesetter Second 60 record holder and has been featured in The Daily, Columns Magazine, and E3. As one of the Top 10 Financial Planners in the country, he currently sits as the Chair of the Financial Plan Automation Committee, helping to usher in the next iteration of software. Having one of the fastest-growing practices in New York City, he holds the Record of Northwestern Mutual's 56-year-old NYC-Midtown Office, which helped attribute to him finishing the 2020 - 2021 Award's Year as the company's New Client Impact Leader, Nationwide.

Jon lives on the Lower East Side in New York City with his wife Elizabeth Taylor, about to celebrate their 3rd wedding anniversary on June 8th, and their two kittens Cheesy Bread (Cheesy) and Crunchwrap Supreme (Crunchy).

WEBSITE: www.jonetaylor.nm.com

EMAIL: jon.e.taylor@nm.com

PHONE: 347-723-7428

GREGORY KOJAK

GREGORY KOJAK, AIF®

Conversation with Gregory Kojak, AIF®

Gregory, you are the Founder of Kojak Capital. Tell us about your work and the people you help.

Gregory Kojak: Post-pandemic, the world changed, and everybody turned in a different direction. Many people had to adjust financially, with their jobs or their children. All of a sudden, expenses crept out of nowhere. So contingency plans had to be built almost immediately. It was a difficult time for many people, and we had to jump right in. Our clients were asking for solutions, so we were helping them and giving them outside perspectives. The silver lining is people are coming out on the other side just fine. They could control their expenses and had more than enough cash and reserves in emergency funds. We could do even more for them and make them even more comfortable with full financial plans and looking at their financials objectively. We help people define goals and project out to see if they will meet those goals. We make adjustments to get them there faster or ensure they don't fall short.

Who are your typical clients?

Gregory Kojak: They run the gamut. I have clients just starting out, newly married couples, and first-time home buyers. I also work with many business owners. We had the most job applications on record in U.S. history during the pandemic because everybody saw opportunities and took advantage of them. So business owners are a big one. There is a whole host of financial issues with business owners about how to structure their companies and build retirement plans for themselves. It's now their responsibility. At the other end of my client list are people in retirement or getting close to retirement. They want to know if they have taken the proper steps to get to where they need to be. And more importantly, they want to make sure that they don't run out of money. As our longevity increases, we want to ensure there are enough assets and income to accommodate any expenses, especially end-of-life scenarios where things get really expensive.

What is the difference between wealth planning and wealth management?

Gregory Kojak: About a decade ago, wealth management became a pretty common term. The industry embraced people who already had many assets, and they wanted to work with these individuals. It was a very profitable source for financial advisors. In my practice, going back about a decade, I found that I was working with people on planning for wealth. So we're helping them accumulate, getting a saving strategy in place, and then making projections going forward. Many of our clients are not expecting any sort of inheritance. So it really comes down to making sure they are well-positioned for life, hence the term wealth planning.

Also, some of my business owner clients are looking to exit or sell their companies, and we plan how to do that. What are the taxes involved upon sale? Will that be enough money for them to have a pleasant retirement? Many moving parts come into play. The one thing I've noticed is that we're very customized and time-intensive. Therefore, we have a smaller client population in general. The average advisor at a large brokerage firm has about 300 to 400 clients. Think about all of those phone calls and emails coming in! I have 104 households. I'm able to return phone calls and emails effectively. If one of my clients has a new baby or is presented with a unique business opportunity, I can provide guidance right away. I don't have to say, "Well, let's wait until the fourth quarter because that is my next review meeting with you." So it really distinguishes me to help in two different ways. As we go through life and plan this journey for our clients, that's the active part. But then, I also have enough time to move forward and accommodate any immediate needs my clients might have.

Are there myths or misconceptions that prevent people from getting their finances in order?

Gregory Kojak: The most common issue is that people don't start planning soon enough. When I start with a new client, the boundary lines are very clear that we do not discuss anyone's financials for any reason. It's not allowed by regulation, and it's unethical. We ensure they're very well aware that everything is entirely 100% private. That affords us a really good relationship because, in some instances, people are embarrassed about things like five-figure credit card bills. They just want to know how to take care of it. Taking the first step is the hardest. And after that, they get that weight off their shoulders and say, "Alright, I'm glad we addressed this because I've been avoiding it for so long." We can create some comfort for our clients, develop a plan and take care of any outstanding bad debt. After that, you take the money going towards that and build towards your future. Once you take the first step, many good things start happening after that.

Gregory, what inspired you to get started in the financial services field?

Gregory Kojak: I started as an intern in college. I was 19 and attending the University of Illinois in Champaign. I came home during summer break, Christmas break, and spring break, and I just wanted to do something. And it was a field that I wasn't even studying because I was a political science/economics major. But I got an internship at a local broker-dealer, and I learned about that industry. From then on, it just kind of snowballed. I had a grasp of returns and performance and an understanding of the mechanics of investments and how they worked. It just blossomed into something that I was more drawn to.

The final element is the interaction with our clients. It's a very special, meaningful relationship. I can't even tell you about one single unruly or difficult client that I have because they're all fantastic. They see the value of our work; they know that they can count on us to return phone calls, engage them and help them with their problems, and ultimately get a financial solution. I'm very blessed to be a part of their whole life. I can't tell you how many times I've been invited to a baptism or a bar mitzvah or had someone call and ask, "Greg, where do you buy your tires from?" They are very close relationships. And again, we're working on some really interesting scenarios where I had Grandma and Grandpa as clients, and they passed away. And now we're working with Mom and Dad on assets and investing money for grandchildren. I get the pleasure of being part of three-generational family planning. It's been fantastic to see the families evolve and grow and their comfort level of knowing exactly where they are with their financials because of the education we provide.

What should people look for when choosing a financial advisor?

Gregory Kojak: There's a couple of different metrics. And it really comes down to what scope of work you need to be done. The financial plan is the actual nitty-gritty, the blueprint for where you want to go, and not all financial advisors offer the financial plan that we do. There's also the asset management portion. Once you have the blueprint and are ready to build the house, you need to hire the workers and buy the materials. And so that's where we build our portfolios to mirror how we're going to get there. There are different elements of risk with your investments. There are various elements of volatility, and those need to be addressed.

You should also make sure that you check out your financial advisor's permanent record through www.finra.org. You can see disclosures, issues with clients, how they were resolved, and things of that nature on the website. Do your due diligence and look at backgrounds.

Finally, just have an honest conversation about what you can expect and what costs are involved. Find out how many clients they have. As I said, some advisors have 500 clients, while those with 100 will have a lot more time. Don't be afraid to ask personal and professional questions. People are often interested in what charitable endeavors I am a part of, as well as my philosophies on passive versus active management. Conversations usually sway between personal and professional topics to see if we are a good match. This is a partnership. Most of my clients understand they are a critical component because I can make recommendations, but they ultimately have to take action and do the homework.

How can people find you, connect with you, and learn more?

Gregory Kojak: My website is www.KojakCapital.com, where you can find all of my contact information. I grew a Covid beard, and it turns out my wife really loves it, so I look a little different in the website videos! Also, I write a monthly newsletter, and I am happy to add people to that list when they sign up online. I talk about the markets, economics, and all sorts of economic and market happenings. I also include pictures of my three kids. Many of my clients love seeing the activities they do between music, sports, and family vacations that we take together. I want my clients to feel like part of my family.

GREGORY KOJAK, AIF®

Founder

KOJAK CAPITAL, Wealth Planning for Life®

On a cold February day in Champaign, Illinois, while working on the infamous U of IL CHEM 205 Cobalt Lab, Greg realized that he was not made to study chemistry for the rest of his life. That analytical skillset led him into economics and finance and he has never looked back; however, he did not abandon it completely. His wife, Karen, was also an undergraduate chemistry major (and finished her chemistry degree!), so some say that they have good chemistry.

Greg's role at Kojak Capital is to serve as a decision-maker for his clients with respect to their ongoing investment management, tax strategy, estate planning, and risk management. These decisions are then implemented and reviewed by Greg and other Kojak Capital staff. Greg's attention has been increasingly dedicated to sophisticated tax strategies as a result of recent tax law changes. He has helped his clients position themselves to avoid being deluged by the wave of future tax increases. His work includes giving presentations to tax professionals, publishing articles on charitable trusts, designing complex IRS qualified and nonqualified plans, and incorporating captive insurance companies for his business-owner clients.

Greg serves as a Chairman of the Board of Directors of the Polish American Association. He is currently the chairman and oversees the organization's $2.5 million budget and 26 programs involving immigration, English as a second language, domestic violence, and substance abuse. It is the largest and oldest social services organization in Chicago that serves the diverse immigrant community. His involvement in the Polish American community resulted in an invitation to attend a non-press leadership conference at the White House in May 2016. A select group of leaders was invited to discuss immigration, NATO, and the Visa Waiver Program candidly with White House officials.

Greg and Karen are the proud parents of ten-year-old "cutie" Claire, born just after St. Patrick's Day in 2011, nine-year-old "smiley" son Ben born on a blazing hot day in July 2012, and their third child Caroline born in a snowy blizzard in March 2015. Claire is enjoying her travel soccer, cross country, and voice lessons. Ben is scoring goals in lacrosse games and jamming with his Thursday night band, Wrecked. Caroline is constantly looking for adventures, being the neighborhood pack leader and in the same soccer club as her older sister Claire. Greg says that weekends are the best part of the week as there is no shortage of activity around his house! To prove that point, Greg was asked to head the cross country and track programs at the kids' school, so any given afternoon, he can be seen with a pack of 60 or so kids running around their school neighborhoods. Their newest furry family addition, named Bruno, came in September 2019. Bruno is a cuddly two-year-old black Labrador and is often seen jogging through the neighborhood with Karen!

EMAIL: Greg@KojakCapital.com

PHONE: (773) 572-6455

WEBSITE: www.KojakCapital.com

ERIC A. DUPRÉ

ERIC A. DUPRÉ

Conversation with Eric A. Dupré

Eric, you are the President of Dupré Financial Group based in San Antonio, Texas. Tell us about your work and the people you help.

Eric A. Dupré: We work with high net worth individuals with at least a million dollars in investable assets. Our work encompasses looking at each client's entire financial picture, whether that be portfolio management, retirement planning, company 401K, life insurance, auto insurance, or health insurance. We are a one-stop shop for our affluent clientele.

How has the recent pandemic impacted the financial services industry?

Eric A. Dupré: Though it hasn't affected our clientele, the pandemic has undoubtedly impacted the industry as a whole. We manage individual portfolios, and the stock market has continued to move to new all-time highs from the pandemic low of March 2020. Last year was a very good year for the stock market. This year has been very good for our investment portfolios, despite the recent volatility.

Are there any common myths and misconceptions in your field?

Eric A. Dupré: There are quite a few naysayers out there who constantly try to scare people into thinking the stock market is going to crash. But the bottom line is that corporate earnings drive the stock market. Last year during the pandemic, even though we had people quarantining and working from home, corporate earnings went up through online shopping. As the vaccines came out and things started opening up again, it continued to bolster the economy through in-person shopping, eating at restaurants, and ordering more goods and services. We have even seen a global supply chain backup, proving that the consumer-driven economy of the United States is very strong.

What mistakes do you help your clients avoid?

Eric A. Dupré: I have encountered people with knee-jerk reactions to the stock market. The volatility that we have seen recently has caused fear in some of our clients, and they wonder whether or not they should get out of the stock market. As I always tell them, the market doesn't like uncertainty. With the new Omnicron variant emerging, there is uncertainty. But it is not a reason to get out of the market and panic. I always advise my clients to stay the course.

Eric, how did you get started in the financial services industry?

Eric A. Dupré: Well, I'm a legacy advisor. My father was in the financial services industry for several years. In 1994, he asked me to consider joining him in the business, and I did. I had the pleasure of working with him until his retirement in 2014. Since then, I have been out on my own.

What should people look for when choosing a financial advisor?

Eric A. Dupré: Look at the advisor's tenure and do your due diligence by talking to several advisors. This is a relationship business, so you want to work with someone you feel comfortable with who has proper education and credentials behind their name. It's never too late to start. But if you can, start early. Develop a plan with your advisor to set some goals and investment objectives. Visit them regularly to ensure you are on track to achieve those goals.

How can people find you, connect with you, and learn more?

Eric A. Dupré: Our website is www.duprefinancialgroup.com. You can also reach us at 210-504-4300. Pick up the phone, and let's have a chat.

ERIC A. DUPRÉ

President

Dupré Financial Group

Eric Dupré is a recognized financial voice in the San Antonio community, having served as the investment professional on the KENS AM 1160 noon business program and appearing as a guest columnist in the Banking & Finance section of the San Antonio Business Journal.

Eric's true professional passion is providing customized financial guidance for you. As the co-portfolio manager of the group, Eric is steadfast in his commitment to helping you pursue your financial goals as he follows in his father's footsteps in the financial services industry.

A native and current resident of San Antonio, Eric is in tune with the values of the community. He enjoys life here with his wife, Priscilla, and sons, Evan and Dylan, and is very active serving others. Eric is a board member of Las Casas Foundation, a member of the Texas Biomedical Research Institute Founder's Council, a current member of Los Compadres de San Antonio Missions, and a past board member of the Baptist Health System Foundation, where he served as chairman of the Leaders Council.

Eric holds the APMA (Accredited Portfolio Management Advisor) & AIF (Accredited Investment Fiduciary) designations.

WEBSITE: www.duprefinancialgroup.com

PHONE: 210-504-4300

ADAM D. KOOS

ADAM D. KOOS, CFP®, CMT®, CEPA

Conversation with Adam D. Koos, CFP®, CMT®, CEPA

Adam, you are a Senior Financial Advisor and President of Libertas Wealth Management Group based in Columbus, Ohio. Tell us about your work and the people you help.

Adam D. Koos: We are a full-service fiduciary and registered investment advisory firm. We're one of the few fiduciaries in the country. Our primary purpose is financial planning and investment management for first-generation business owners looking to sell their company in the future, as well as C-suite, D-suite, SVP, and VP executives.

What specific challenges do your clients face?

Adam D. Koos: The executives working for big Fortune 500 companies face the challenge of ensuring their families are taken care of if something happens to them. People often don't want to talk about this morbid topic, and it may not seem like a big problem. But it is actually the *biggest* problem.

In addition, they have to deal with complicated benefits packages, stock options, etc. Those can be confusing enough on their own, but you also have to combine them with financial planning, retirement planning, and tax planning so that it all makes sense.

Finally, the biggest concern, which most business owners don't even realize, is that they can sell their companies someday. For those who think they can sell, many aren't aware of all the work they can do to increase the company's value. The saddest statistic is that more than 75% of business owners regret selling one year later because they did no personal financial planning prior to starting their exit planning and value acceleration. It's almost like life after football. When you're finished playing in the pros, you don't know what to do with your life when you're done with football. It is the same with business owners, except they are 65 years old. How do they get something for the business they spent years creating and bundling, and what do they do when they ultimately exit from the role they've been performing - likely for decades - when it's time to pass the metaphorical baton?

Do business owners understand the importance of financial planning? Do you ever see them trying to do it on their own?

Adam D. Koos: I don't think business owners are looking for it. They are too busy running their businesses, managing their staff, and growing their companies. So I don't believe they spend a lot of time looking. I'm speaking from experience because I've been there. Many highly successful entrepreneurs are just looking for a simple way to do financial planning on their own, and they assume that their business will be their "retirement plan." But so few - and I mean, VERY few actually assess the value of their business today to determine what it's worth, not to mention how they can increase its value.

And thankfully, in hindsight, since the stock market hasn't taken a drop in value that hasn't recovered in more than four months for the past 13 to 14 years now, it's perceivably easy to do, right? Now, when we have the next mortgage crisis, tech bubble, or apocalypse, that will probably change.

I think 70% to 80% of people out there just don't know what to ask. They don't know what to look for. I always say there is nothing wrong with looking for the unicorn of retirement planning and doing it on your own. But you need two things. First, you have to be interested in it. And second, you need the time. And if you don't have the interest, you won't spend the time. And even if you do have the interest, some people just don't have the time because they have kids and families and just a lot going on. We always joke at our office, "This is why we have a job!"

What are some questions that everyone should ask about financial planning?

Adam D. Koos: How much should I be saving? It doesn't take a rocket scientist to know that the earlier you start, the better off you are. And the more you save, the better off you are. Nobody wants to live paycheck to paycheck and not have fun during their working years. So you shouldn't do that, of course. But ask yourself, "How much do I need to save to make work optional someday?" This is not to say you ***have*** to quit, but it would be nice to have the option to walk in one day and say you were leaving if you felt the need.

When it comes to 401Ks, most people say, "Well, my match is dollar for dollar up to 4%. So I'm just going to put away 4%."

Or, "Oh, I got a bonus this year, so I will put away 6% now." But there is no real end game in mind. It's like they are just putting money away because somebody told them it was the right thing to do.

Another important question to consider is, "What would happen to my family if I were gone? How would they replace that income?" Often, we see people in their late 50s who don't have enough insurance. And by the way, as a fiduciary, I don't even sell insurance, but these people are ready to quit working, and they're not even thinking about the fact that a long-term care facility costs $9,000 a month today in middle-America. You have to plan for that. Some people are great planners, but I don't think that most people are.

What mistakes do you help your clients avoid?

Adam D. Koos: Not starting the planning process early enough, not saving enough, and thinking the match (on their 401k) is all they need to put away for themselves. Another mistake would be not analyzing their income to determine if putting money in a traditional pre-tax 401k or a Roth would make the most sense. I've been seeing more and more people putting money into the Roth thinking, "Oh, well, I've got some pre-tax money; I think I will have some after-tax money now." That seems to balance in their head, but really, they are leaving tons of money on the table and giving it to the IRS.

At the end of the day, THE biggest mistake investors make is not having a written comprehensive plan… a roadmap that says what you are spending today, saving today, and future expenses. How often are you going to want a new car or a vacation when you're retired? How often will you go on road trips to visit family? And how much is all of that going to cost? It is essential to extrapolate into the future and know you are saving enough to do all of the things on your bucket list.

The fact is that most people do not have a financial plan. Most companies probably charge a hard dollar fee for it. So it is difficult for people to fork over $2,000 to $3,000 for a plan. We don't charge a hard dollar for plans at our office, but most firms do. The bottom line is, even if you failed to start planning early, once your kids leave the house and you are in your 50s or 60s, you need to have a plan. Most people don't, and that's a huge mistake.

Adam, what inspired you to get started in the financial services field?

Adam D. Koos: It's a long story, but I will give you the Cliffs Notes version. I grew up watching my dad, who was an optometrist. I would stop at his office on my way home from school every day, and I would see how much his staff and patients loved him and what a great culture he had in his office. I wanted to have that culture one day. I loved medicine. I shadowed him at work once, and he saw 12 to 14 patients, asking all of them the same thing. "Which one can you see more clearly? This one, or that one? This one, or that one?" He did this over and over again, and it just didn't seem that exciting to me.

So I went to college. I knew I wanted to get into medicine, and I went down the trauma surgery track. And to make a very long story short, I competed in Taekwondo way back in the day, roughly 70 pounds ago, as I always say (as a joke). At that time, fighting kept me focused on school and studying. I ended up with a career-ending injury my junior year, and after that, I just wanted to make up for lost time, so I decided that I didn't want to go to school for seven more years and had to figure out a new career path.

My dad said to me, "I know you don't want to be a doctor anymore. What do you think about being a 'financial surgeon' instead?" He introduced me to his financial advisor, and I still wasn't totally enthralled with the whole idea. But once I saw you could make huge impacts on people's lives and build multi-decade relationships with them, all while making a good living, I was sold.

It seemed like a no-brainer. So, here I am, 20+ years later, and while I don't have an optometry practice and I don't have patients, per se, I do have a wonderful family of clients, I love my staff, and I always say that I feel like I haven't worked in two decades.

What should people look for when choosing a financial advisor?

Adam D. Koos: The first thing is trust, and trust is a very individual thing. We recently had a prospective client reach out to us, asking to go to happy hour (twice now, actually), just to talk and get to know who I am, who we are, and how we would work with them long-term. We haven't even gotten into the process of initiating a discovery meeting, education meeting, and financial planning meeting. This person is still trying to decide if they like me and whether or not they can trust me. So trust is a big one, I'd say, but also probably the toughest.

To be completely selfless here and provide everyone reading, listening, or watching with some authentic, free advice, go to www.napfa.org and type in your zip code. It will pull up all of the fiduciaries in your area. A fiduciary is a financial advisory firm that has dropped all of its brokerage licenses, which means it cannot legally accept a commission. This eliminates the vast majority of the conflicts of interest that exist in the financial advisory and financial planning world. So, after you've done this little bit of research, you'll and up faced with the top 8% of firms in the country, just based on conflict-free advice. From there, 90% of your research is done. Choose three or four, interview them, and decide who you would get along with best.

How do people find you, connect with you, and learn more?

Adam D. Koos: Our website is www.LibertasWealth.com. You can send us a message or set up a 20-minute intro call to determine if we might be a good fit now or in the future. My email address is adam@LibertasWealth.com. If anyone wants to contact me directly... you never have to be a client to ask a question, and I'm always happy to be a sounding board. I've been very fortunate all my life - I love my job, so answering questions for those who are enthusiastically interested in bettering themselves financially... I'm always willing to help!

ADAM D. KOOS, CFP®, CMT®, CEPA

Senior Financial Adviser and President

Libertas Wealth Management Group, Inc.

Adam was born in Oberlin, Ohio, to Kim and Stephen Koós, during "The Blizzard of '78." His mom is the daughter of Irish and German parents, and his dad was born in Györ, Hungary, and escaped the country during the communist revolution with his siblings and parents in 1956.

The oldest of four children, Adam was always very ambitious, passionate, giving and generous – and he always knew that someday he would make a significant impact in the lives of others.

He moved to Columbus in 1996 to attend college at The Ohio State University, where he met his best friend and bride, Donna. Shortly after graduation, at the 2002 Ohio State vs. m*ch*g*n game, Adam arranged for The Ohio State Marching Band to surround he and his bride-to-be outside St. John's Arena, where he dropped to a knee and proposed. They were married in June of 2003 and after seven fun, independent, child-free years, they opened up a new chapter in their lives with two amazing boys, Karston & Kamden.

When he's not being the best father and husband he can be, Adam loves sitting outside, watching thunderstorms come in, or soaking in the very few dry, 70-degree days that central Ohio has to offer. A lifetime "car guy," he enjoys taking Karston and Kamden to gawk at elite and/or restored cars, alongside his sponsorship of Columbus Cars & Coffee, as well as his newly-founded organization, "Kars for Kids," a non-profit that holds events for kids who've lost a parent, giving them the opportunity to ride in their "dream car."

While we all know time is a scarce commodity, Adam enjoys playing sand volleyball year-round with Donna and their friends, tries to get a game of golf or tennis in a few times each summer, and is an extremely passionate football fan. In fact, he has attended more than 120 home Buckeye games since 1995 and has been a relentless supporter of the Cleveland Browns through thick and thin!

Adam started his career in 2001, just ten days before the World Trade Center was attacked, which means he's had the fortunate experience of helping his clients through three of the worst stock market crashes in U.S. history.

He holds the elite CERTIFIED FINANCIAL PLANNERTM certification, is one of only 3,000+ Chartered Market Technicians (CMT) in the world, is a Certified Financial Technician (CFTe) through the international federation of Technical Analysts, and a Certified Exit Planning Advisor (CEPA), helping entrepreneurs and business owners to make work "optional" and exit their companies in a profitable, tax-efficient manner.

- Locally, Adam has been named one of central Ohio's "20 People to Know in Finance" by Business First,
- Is a recipient of the 2011 Business First Greater Columbus "Forty Under 40" award,
- A 6-time winner of Columbus CEO Magazine's "Best of Business" awards (winning "Best Private Wealth Management Firm"),
- Has been named one of central Ohio's "Top Fee-Only Financial Planning Firms" by Business First every year since 2014,
- The piece of recognition he's *most proud of* is being named a winner of the Better Business Bureau "Torch Award for Ethics & Trust."

In addition to all the recognition he's received here in Ohio, Adam has also been nationally recognized by:

- Financial Advisor Magazine as one of only eight portfolio managers chosen to their "Research All-Star Team" for research and investment management.
- Investopedia named him as one of the top-100 Most Influential Financial Advisors in the U.S.
- Proactive Advisor Magazine interviewed and featured him on the cover of their magazine with a focus on his Defense First® investment management strategy.

Adam spends the majority of his time assisting clients with high-level, complex financial, retirement, and estate planning needs, as well as managing all of our corporate and individual client investment portfolios.

Raised in a family of teachers, he has become an accomplished speaker, writer, and educator, providing financial planning classes, "401(k) Boot Camps," and many other programs and workshops for individuals, couples, corporations, and organizations, both private and public.

Lastly, Adam is an accomplished columnist. He is a regular contributor to Seeking Alpha and a former contributor to "The Trading Deck" on Wall Street Journal's MarketWatch.com. You can also find his columns in Forbes, US News & World Report, Yahoo! Finance, Fox Business, Investopedia, and many others. Locally, he has either been interviewed by, or written articles for Columbus Business First, The Columbus Dispatch, Columbus CEO Magazine, and has appeared several times on WBNS 10TV.

WEBSITE: www.libertaswealth.com

EMAIL: adam@libertaswealth.com

JACOB CHRYSLER

JACOB CHRYSLER, CFP®, CKA®

Conversation with Jacob Chrysler, CFP®, CKA®

Jacob, you are a Certified Financial Planner and Certified Kingdom Advisor in central Ohio. Tell us about your work and the people you help.

Jacob Chrysler: Our clients are looking to live at the intersection of faith and finance. We believe some key biblical principles undergird many financial decisions we make daily and over our lifetime. So we're passionate about helping people live their best life at the intersection of faith and finance.

How has the recent pandemic impacted the financial services industry?

Jacob Chrysler: As far as communication goes, you have to be comfortable using a computer. This new virtual world is uncomfortable for many retirees or people approaching retirement age. Before the pandemic, most people only used their phones for entertainment purposes. Now we are reliant on technology to communicate, make financial transactions, and other interactions that we were used to having in person.

Secondly, people are more fearful. They are more willing to keep a lot of money in their bank account because they feel it is "safe." And the conversations that we're having with clients are, "Is that something that really makes sense for you? Are you acting out of fear? Or is there a reason behind the amount of cash that you have?" We are big preachers of being ready for emergencies. The story of the ant saving food for winter is something that we love, but there's a limit to it, and we don't want to live in fear. So it has been a matter of just trying to help our clients work through this new world.

Are there myths or misconceptions that prevent people from getting their finances in order?

Jacob Chrysler: The first one is that you need to have it all together to get started. Most people that have it all together don't really need our services. We're here to help people who are messy, fearful, and who don't have all of their questions answered. Hopefully, we can meet those people where they are and move them forward. The folks who are doing it themselves and are successful may not find value in what we do unless they are growing tired of keeping up with the ever-changing world of finance and want to delegate that responsibility to an advisor. We're not looking for the people that have it all together. We're looking for the people that need help.

Another misconception is that things are how they have always been and always will be. I think we misapply this common axiom to the stock market, jobs, and family situations. On a personal note, we've lost some of our favorite clients this year to the pandemic. And so for many of our clients, the holidays are very different. With that comes many financial planning questions and conversations that people probably didn't anticipate. We just want to be there and be alongside them in those times.

What mistakes do you help your clients avoid?

Jacob Chrysler: People don't fully understand their workplace benefits. I can't tell you how many times I've gone through a pay stub and seen benefits that people didn't know they applied for during open enrollment. Now, they're paying every two weeks for stuff they don't even need. On the other hand, they may not have all the coverage they could get through their workplace plan.

Another pitfall, specifically on the protection side of things, is people don't understand how much their life insurance and disability insurance through work is costing them compared to a policy they can get on the open market. An additional misconception people have is how much is going into their health savings account. Health care is a huge issue right now. Many companies use health savings accounts to help fund their employees' healthcare expenses. Folks don't always understand how much they're putting in versus what their company is putting in versus the level premium for having the coverage. When expenses arise, there can be surprises. People don't always understand how much is available in their plan and how to leverage the health savings account after they are done working.

Jacob, what inspired you to get started in the financial services industry?

Jacob Chrysler: I love answering this question. My grandfather was a farmer and took out quite a bit of debt, as many farmers do. To protect my grandmother if something happened to him, he took out a significant life insurance policy so she could pay off any debts the farm had. Eventually, he realized that he didn't want to be a farmer anymore. In time, he built a successful second career as a stockbroker and paid off his farm debt. Having achieved financial independence, he decided to keep the insurance policy in place. Unfortunately, he developed cancer just a couple of years later and passed away. This sounds like a sad story, but it isn't. I heard it for the first time in college. It was then I realized that after he died, my grandfathers' insurance money allowed my grandma to be the "Mimi" that I loved so much. She took us on trips, went with us to sporting events, was always there for her children and grandchildren, and was a very financially generous person. With appreciation and inspiration, I started taking more business and finance classes and eventually became a financial planner.

What should people look for when choosing a financial advisor?

Jacob Chrysler: Number one, find someone you trust. There are many different ways to develop trust. Secondly, there are guardrails in place to help determine which financial advisors are bound by a fiduciary standard. Are you looking for a transactional relationship? Or someone who will be proactive and act in your best interest? If the latter, you want to find a Certified Financial Planner® because we have taken an oath to uphold the fiduciary standard and act in our client's best interest even if it hurts our bottom line. Think of it as a lawyer or CPA; they will give you advice in your best interest regardless of whether or not they win the case or you get a tax refund.

We're there for our clients. We view this as a serious profession of giving advice based on the client's individual circumstances. "One size fits all" is not something we are familiar with. Everyone we sit in front of has a reason for being there. And that reason is specific to them.

How can people find you, connect with you, and learn more?

Jacob Chrysler: Our website is www.bestlifefg.com. You can also reach out to me directly on LinkedIn. If you are still having trouble finding me, you can narrow your internet browser search to Columbus, Ohio, Certified Kingdom Advisors, and I'm sure I will be near the top.

JACOB CHRYSLER, CFP®, CKA®

Certified Financial Planner and Certified Kingdom Advisor

Jake is passionate about guiding individuals and families who want to live at the intersection of faith and finance. He resides in Bellefontaine, OH, with his wife, Alayna, and son, Calvin.

WEBSITE: www.bestlifefg.com

LINKEDIN: Jacob Chrysler

MICHAEL CHRISLER

MICHAEL CHRISLER

Conversation with Michael Chrisler

Michael, you are the Founder of MJC Financial Fitness. Tell us about your work and the people you help.

Michael Chrisler: Over the years, I worked with many advisors at a financial technology firm. I found that younger families and people just starting in their careers didn't have access to advisors. So I decided to start MJC Financial Fitness. I'm a little different than a typical advisor because I don't have a minimum asset level required to work with me. I'm looking to help out and grow with people during their financial journey. I've always had a deep love for financial literacy and helping people navigate the waters of the finance system because that system is not always set up for people to succeed.

Is there a benefit to starting financial planning early in life?

Michael Chrisler: Definitely. I have worked with folks in their 30's and 40's. But if I could catch someone in their 20's, right out of college or just starting out in their career, that magical compound interest could do some amazing things. It's essential to have someone in your corner to help you determine what to invest in and how to work with your employer benefits. But another thing I really strive for is a judgment-free zone. If you are in your 40's or 50's, you're still young. And if you haven't started saving yet, we'll start from where you are and build from there. The past is the past, and the future is the future.

Are there any challenges that prevent people from getting their finances in order?

Michael Chrisler: The younger you can start, the better. Time is a huge advantage. There are many exciting investment opportunities with the way the world is right now. People all over social media talk about investing a couple of thousand dollars and turning it into large sums of money. One downside might be as you're investing in the stock market or putting money into your 401k through mutual funds, it's going to grow slowly. As you get older, you kind of lose some of that compound interest, and you may not be able to go as aggressive with some of your investment choices. But anytime is a good time to start for most people. It's all about getting that first dollar in the account. I worked with someone yesterday who had read all about the importance of saving for retirement but didn't know where to start. I enjoy helping people in those situations.

How has the recent pandemic impacted the financial services industry?

Michael Chrisler: One thing I start with for new clients is to make sure they have a liquid emergency fund. And people always wonder, "What exactly is this money for? It's just kind of sitting in a savings account and not earning much interest." But when you go through a pandemic, it becomes easier to understand the importance of having that money set aside. Perhaps you lost your job when your company shut down, or your spouse lost theirs. Maybe the water heater went out and needed to be replaced. If you don't have a job but things around the house still need to be repaired, you need cash to make it happen. So thinking about those things was a positive change in mindset for people.

The pandemic also caused people to reevaluate their careers. Maybe you are putting in too many hours or realizing this isn't exactly what you want to do with your life. So that is another thing I'll work on with folks. "Here's what you're making, and here are your benefits. If you leave now, what does that look like? What do you need to look for to match it or beat it?" And it's not always going to be monetary matching. Happiness is a big factor too. You can make a lot less money, maybe work fewer hours, and just be more fulfilled in life.

Are there common myths or misconceptions about financial planning?

Michael Chrisler: The way I look at it, we are investing for the long-term. Are there people who have these great investments that turn into millions or billions of dollars? Sure. But don't think that applies to everyone who is saving for something. I still stand behind a low-cost index fund approach, kind of investing in the whole market. I avoid getting into the nitty-gritty of, "This person says this stock is going to go up. This person over here loves this particular cryptocurrency." And all that being said, I stay up on all the trends. If I get a question about digital assets or any type of new investment, I want to have a well-formed opinion or be somewhat versed in the subject. Could cryptocurrency be part of a portfolio? Definitely, but should it be part of every portfolio? Probably not.

What mistakes do you help your clients avoid?

Michael Chrisler: Many of the mistakes I experienced personally. When I came out of college, I had a huge amount of credit card debt. That can really put a dent in someone's saving future. Imagine paying a bank 18% to 20% per year. Sometimes that minimum payment doesn't cover the interest fees, depending on your balance. So that's something to keep an eye on.

Also, don't fall victim to those sneaky subscriptions. They won't ruin your retirement, but things like Netflix and other subscription services on your credit card can really add up. And we don't tend to look at those very often.

In addition, I don't advise constantly moving investments around or changing them frequently. When we begin the investing process, we develop a plan, and we need to let the plan and the market do their thing. Yes, the market is volatile, but we expect that and keep our eye on the end goal.

These are all common missteps, but nothing that can't be fixed.

Michael, what inspired you to get started in the financial services field?

Michael Chrisler: I had great financial role models. My parents were very good with money. We didn't have an abundance of it, but we never felt like it wasn't enough. My parents did well with saving and budgeting. And somehow, even with their great example, I still came out of college spending money like crazy. I'm definitely a spender; my wife is a saver. I work with my clients to figure out which one they are and develop a plan from there.

It certainly can be stressful right out of college as you try to juggle rent, bills, and attempt to figure out the benefits attached to your new job. As I worked with my first few clients, I saw that they were paying fees for their checking accounts or credit card interest. Most of them had not taken a look at their insurance at all. It's nice to have someone in your corner just to say, "Hey, let's move this checking account somewhere else because paying $15 a month to this bank doesn't really make any sense." Financial literacy and helping folks just starting out were my most significant reasons for entering the field.

What should people look for when choosing a financial advisor?

Michael Chrisler: You need to feel comfortable with the person you choose. A one-on-one connection is something you may not get with the larger firms. They may be less expensive, but you might not get the same advisor every time, and your calls could be directed to a call center. There's nothing wrong with that, but do you want to pay a little less and sacrifice your individuality? Or spend a little more to develop a specific plan for you and your goals?

I am a fee-only financial advisor. That means I don't get any commissions on the products I sell. So I feel like that is a crucial thing to consider. Along with being fee-only, I am also a fiduciary; this means that when I offer advice, it must be in your best interest. Being with a fiduciary allows you to feel comfortable that your advisor is making the best recommendation for you.

How can people find you, connect with you, and learn more?

Michael Chrisler: My website is www.mjcfinancialfitness.com. You can take a look at the products and services I offer, as well as set up a quick consultation to meet me and talk about your goals. You can find my email address on the website as well. I want to make sure that everyone reading knows that I am here to help (no matter your current financial situation) and even if we don't end up working together, I want to provide value to you.

MICHAEL CHRISLER

Founder

MJC Financial Fitness

MJC Financial Fitness founder Michael Chrisler is an experienced advisor, having spent nearly 15 years working in the financial technology industry. During that time he trained thousands of advisors on how to effectively use technology to create a better client experience. The importance of offering clients a full financial wellness picture was always stressed.

Today he is able to take that experience and use it to help his clients as a fee-only financial advisor. He's particularly passionate about helping young families and creative freelancers — people he often saw overlooked by financial advisors in the past. His goal is to make financial planning more accessible and less scary, so his clients can start building towards the life they want. Michael is a member of the XY Planning Network, National Association of

Personal Financial Planners (NAPFA), and the Fee-Only Advisor Network.

Michael lives in Chicago with his wife Brittany and their two sons. Michael enjoys spending quality time playing video games with his sons, practicing martial arts, and being the IT support for his entire family.

WEBSITE: www.mjcfinancialfitness.com

PHONE: 312-764-1160

EMAIL: mchrisler@mjcfinancialfitness.com

LINKEDIN: https://www.linkedin.com/in/mchrisler/

SHANNA TINGOM

SHANNA TINGOM, AAMS®, CFDA®

Conversation with Shanna Tingom, AAMS®, CFDA®

Shanna, you are the co-founder of Heritage Financial Strategies. Tell us about your work and the people you help.

Shanna Tingom: We do financial planning for a flat annual fee for those folks that need help with major life decisions or just want to "adult" better. Some people want to make better decisions today, while others have goals for pre-retirement up to and including retirement. We help people make the hard decisions and even the "not so hard" decisions. We act as the devil and the angel on their shoulder, if you will, as they work their way through life.

We also help manage assets, and we charge a percentage of the assets that we manage. But there's no requirement for one or the other in our practice - it's really up to you! So you can do either one or both. Our clients like the flexibility of choosing how they work with us.

What types of challenges do your clients face?

Shanna Tingom: Well, many of our clients are in the sandwich generation. They are raising children and trying to get them off to college, all while mom and dad need more and more help. And they're trying to balance those two very diverse goals while ensuring their retirement is still on track. We help folks balance those two things. Our goal is to do it in a way that makes everybody happy and creates a win-win scenario for each family member involved.

How has the recent pandemic impacted the financial services industry?

Shanna Tingom: We were making virtual appointments even before virtual appointments were cool, so we have clients all over the country because of that. The pandemic shifted many of our clients away from wanting to come into the office. And even if they're a mile and a half down the street, some of them are opting to see us virtually because it's more convenient, and they can do it during the workday without taking off. So we have many more clients coming to us who are more comfortable meeting virtually. And some of those clients want to retire earlier than they thought they did pre-pandemic because the last couple of years have been rough on a lot of us. So they're looking for a way to retire a little bit earlier, maybe enter that encore career, or volunteer before they fully retire. The pandemic has shifted mindsets for many people.

Are there myths or misconceptions that prevent people from getting their finances in order?

Shanna Tingom: People think they must have millions of dollars to need a financial planner. That just isn't true. We can help you get to the point where you have millions of dollars. Anyone who wants to learn how to manage their money, manage their investments, and better understand where their cash and investments are headed can benefit from the help of a great firm such as ours.

What mistakes do you help your clients avoid?

Shanna Tingom: One of the most common is taking the advice of their HR department or a friend regarding what workplace investment to choose, whether it is a 401K, 403B, or 457 plan. People don't get excellent advice at work. They tend to do the "eeny, meeny, miny, moe" and pick the ones that look the best. And while those might not be bad investments, they might not be the best investments for them. Also, some companies are lucky enough to have a Roth 401K and a traditional 401K. We often see people completely ignore the Roth side, and that is an absolute tragedy because that money comes out and is taxed at the end when it could have been taxed going in at a much lower amount. So we help people choose the right workplace plan because it is the most significant investment and asset for most of us, and it is not a "one size fits all" for everyone. Age and income play into which plan is the best one for you, and getting the wrong advice could have a negative impact 10, 20, or even 30 years down the road when you are getting ready to retire.

Shanna, what inspired you to get started in the financial services field?

Shanna Tingom: I was a secondary music ed major going into college. So this is a huge departure from where I thought I wanted to be when I was in high school. I was the kid in remedial math in school, though my clients probably didn't want to hear that! But math is not my strong suit. So when I ended up in the financial services industry, it was a shock to my family, for sure. But I have loved it for the last 30 years.

The way I was treated when I wanted to learn more about investing and saving inspired me to get involved in this industry. I was in college, working five jobs to pay my way through, and I made an appointment with a local financial advisor in my small town in Iowa. I went in and sat down with him, and I said, "Listen, I don't have any money right now. Someday I hope to, but I don't right now. Help me because I want to learn." My parents were Depression-era kids, and their idea of investing was savings and CDs at the bank. I knew that wouldn't get me to where I needed to go. He set his pen down, reached across the desk, patted me on the head, and said, "Don't worry, sweetheart, someday your husband will take care of this for you." That moment changed my life. I got pissed. I started reading books and learning to do things on my own. Within a few months, I changed my major to business. That really set me on the trajectory of doing what I do today.

We are not the traditional financial planning firm; we are much more casual. We're much more about conversations and how this affects you versus the beta and the alpha of the investments that we offer. We have all of the letters behind our names, but we care more about you and how what we're proposing will impact you now and in the future. And that all stems back to the conversation I had almost 30 years ago now.

What should people look for when choosing a financial advisor?

Shanna Tingom: I compare our relationships with our clients to a marriage. You have to really like the advisor and the firm they work for because it is a long-term arrangement. The longer you work with your advisor, the more successful you will be in achieving your financial goals and having your investments match those goals. You want to take your time to do your due diligence on the front end. You should enjoy talking with your advisor and understand what they are saying to you. And you've got to leave that meeting with a warm and fuzzy feeling. If those things don't exist, it will not be a fulfilling relationship on both ends. So to me, that's the most important thing. When I'm looking at bringing in clients to our firm, we want to make sure that we enjoy working with them because life is just too short not to.

How do people find you, connect with you, and learn more?

Shanna Tingom: Our website is heritagefinancialaz.com if you want to read our blogs, listen to our podcasts, or learn more about how we work. Visit talktoHFS.com to schedule a time to speak with me or any of the wonderful advisors on my team. If you are in the Phoenix metro area, Tucson, or Albuquerque, we can meet you in person. If you are anywhere else in the country, we would love to meet with you virtually.

Securities offered through Registered Representatives of Cambridge Investment Research, Inc., a broker dealer, member FINRA/SIPC. Advisory services offered through Cambridge Investment Research Advisors, Inc., a Registered Investment Adviser. Cambridge and Heritage Financial Strategies are not affiliated.

SHANNA TINGOM, AAMS®, CFDA®

Co-Founder

Heritage Financial Strategies

Shanna Tingom is the co-founder of Heritage Financial Strategies. She has more than 20 years of experience in the financial services industry. She specializes in working with female entrepreneurs, business owners, leaders, and individuals experiencing life transitions such as marriage or divorce. Her primary focus is helping others take charge of their financial future.

After years of struggling to fit into the corporate mold, Shanna became an independent advisor. She earned a bachelor's degree in business from William Penn University and a master's degree in organizational management from the University of Phoenix. Shanna currently holds FINRA Series 7 and 66 licenses and the Accredited Asset Management Specialist℠ and Certified Divorce Financial Analyst designations. She considers herself a life-long learner and keeps apprised of changes in the financial industry. She is currently a Candidate for CFP® certification and hopes to complete certification in 2022.

Since opening Heritage Financial Strategies, Shanna has been a regular contributor to Investopedia.com, Kiplinger's Personal Finance online, and Born2Invest.com. She makes frequent public speaking and guest radio appearances in Phoenix and nationally and hosts her own podcast, "Making Money Fun," which can be found on iTunes.

EMAIL: welcome@heritagefinancialaz.com

PHONE: 480-397-1184

WEBSITE: www.heritagefinancialaz.com

FACEBOOK: https://www.facebook.com/HeritageFinancialStrategies

INSTAGRAM: @stingom

TWITTER: @stingom

OTHER: talktohfs.com to schedule a consultation

GABRIELLE KELLY

GABRIELLE KELLY, CPA

Conversation with Gabrielle Kelly, CPA

Gabrielle, you are a Co-Founder of WEM. Tell us about your work and the people you help.

Gabrielle Kelly: We help give mom-entrepreneurs cash flow management tools to build their business to serve them by increasing their profitability and saving them time. We support them professionally and personally to make sure that their business gives them the lives they dreamed of when first starting out. We know that mom-entrepreneurs have historically been underserved in the finance world, so we're here to change that narrative.

What does WEM stand for?

Gabrielle Kelly: "We Empower Mom-entrepreneurs." Simple and powerful!

What challenges do your clients face?

Gabrielle Kelly: Cash flow is a common concern. Many founders we work with are losing sleep and have anxiety about cash flow, whether it be making payroll next week or paying themselves. We have seen a culture in the startup world known as "the grind." Our services include profitability, coaching, and cash flow management to help mom-entrepreneurs choose a different path than the "startup grind." While all entrepreneurs run into this issue, it's even more important that we support mom-entrepreneurs, given the challenges they also face at home. We want them to have less stress in their lives. This is the ultimate balance for the mom entrepreneur.

Are there any common myths or misconceptions founders have about financial planning?

Gabrielle Kelly: We have done workshops on the myth that your profit comes last. Many founders believe that profit is an event that happens when you're all done with the month to see what's leftover for yourself. We help to reteach that your profit can come first, and you can still run the business after paying yourself. Creating goals and achievable baby steps can help change that mindset of treating yourself last (which we know can be the default for moms). We are striving for harmony between a fulfilling career and a happy family.

How has the recent pandemic impacted the financial services industry?

Gabrielle Kelly: One thing has been the "great resignation" where people leave the corporate world and create opportunities for themselves, which is fantastic. We think everybody needs to know that entrepreneurship is an option for them instead of selling themselves into another corporate job. Again, we want to help mom-entrepreneurs avoid the grind of starting their own business to make it an easier transition and achieve their financial goals.

What mistakes do you help your clients avoid?

Gabrielle Kelly: Straying from their north star. Often as mom-entrepreneurs, we do this for our family to have a flexible schedule and provide stability and support we know we deserve. However, it's very easy to get caught up in the "grind" and therefore lose sight of that north star - spending endless hours working on the business and doing the exact opposite of the business's goal. We ask the questions that help lead back to that north star, "What do you need to support your family financially? How can we build your schedule to align with your family's needs and commitments?" Then we help set a road map and create financial baby steps to get there. This is our mission. It doesn't have to be a hard choice to make. mom-entrepreneurs can have a successful business AND time for their family, and we want to help them get there.

Gabrielle, what inspired you to get started in the financial services industry?

Gabrielle Kelly: I come from a background in financial auditing and public company accounting. Similar to what is happening with the "great resignation," I found that the corporate world wasn't serving me as a mom. Instead, I was serving the corporate world, stakeholders, and shareholders. With the role I am in now, I use my passion for teaching to help fellow mom-entrepreneurs and create a culture shift in the finance and accounting world to provide more empathy, support, and flexibility, which you don't typically find in traditional finance.

What should people look for when choosing a financial advisor?

Gabrielle Kelly: There are consultants and coaches out there for several things. Look for somebody with your best interests in mind, personally and professionally. Do you connect with them? Do you trust them? Do they give you a good feeling? Do they care more about you than your business financials? Are they available to you when you have questions? Do they have a good network? Your gut is usually a pretty good indicator of whether or not they will be a good fit, just like hiring an employee on your team. The financial advisor you choose to work with needs to be similarly "gut-checked."

How can people find you, connect with you, and learn more?

Gabrielle Kelly: You can reach me by email at hi@wem.co. You can find me on LinkedIn by searching Gabrielle Kelly - CPA. Lastly, we are on Instagram @wemfinancial. We are so excited to help fellow mom-entrepreneurs live their dreams.

GABRIELLE KELLY, CPA

Co-Founder

WEM

Gabbie Kelly is a CPA who has always wanted the finance and accounting industry to be better, treat people better, and work better with mom-entrepreneurs. She co-founded WEM because she believes mom-entrepreneurs deserve to have a system to ensure their profitability and financial success without having to sacrifice 100% of their time with their family, friends, and hobbies to grind it out. Why become an entrepreneur if you never get financial freedom or the freedom to work when and how you want to? Moms do twice the work [dammit!]. Life is about so much more than work.

It's time to give mom-entrepreneurs a system to reward their risk of starting their own business and celebrate all they've achieved (because we all know moms don't celebrate themselves enough).

EMAIL: gabrielle@wem.co

LINKEDIN: https://www.linkedin.com/in/gabriellekelly-cpa

INSTAGRAM: @wemfinancial

MICHAEL P. NELAN

MICHAEL P. NELAN

Conversation with Michael P. Nelan

Michael, you are the President of Fair Oaks Financial, Inc. Tell us about your work and the people you help.

Michael Nelan: Fair Oaks Financial, Inc. is a full-service financial services firm. We're an independent financial advisor and part of the Advisor Group, a huge broker-dealer conglomerate with 12,000 advisors nationwide. But we're small enough to be a boutique if you will. We help our clients meet their financial needs through financial planning, insurance, life insurance, and annuities when it makes sense. Our typical client is a pre-retiree, somebody in their late 40s to early 50s. We also do cash flow planning and investment management for post-retirees.

How has the recent pandemic impacted the financial services industry?

Michael Nelan: I try to look for the good in everything. Obviously, a pandemic is a challenging event. And, of course, we're still dealing with it. The market was down today because of concerns over the new Omicron variant, and rightfully so. Hopefully, it's not a major thing and will be short-lived.

In our business, most in-person meetings have changed to virtual meetings. Before this, it was almost negligible to do virtual meetings. I have clients all over the country in Oregon, Southern California, Arizona, and Nevada. But I would still go and see them personally. So now, from the standpoint of convenience and overall efficiency, we use Zoom meetings. And I think that's made a big difference. Some of the presentation materials can be done much easier via Zoom because I can illustrate certain things and focus on various presentations and reports along with specific recommendations. We can also use eMoney, a major financial planning software program in which my clients can log on and interact with the program in real-time. All of those things have been very positive for the industry.

Are there any myths or misconceptions regarding financial planning?

Michael Nelan: We're in a society where everybody can do it themselves. And I think that is the challenge we have in our business. For example, there are several competitors out there, such as the Schwabs and the TD Ameritrades of the world, along with new players such as Robin Hood. I look at companies such as Robin Hood as an opportunity for individual investors to learn more about what we do and how they learn more about investing. It's helpful to immerse yourself in things like this and know a little bit about how stocks work before you come and meet with us. So I consider it a good thing. I think many people who want to manage their own portfolios will end up doing that anyway. We have the tools and resources to sort out potential investments and find value where your average investor can't. But I think the misconception is that "I can do it myself." And the reality is, I can change a transmission. I have done that. But I don't want to. It's not my expertise.

What mistakes do you help clients avoid?

Michael Nelan: We have clients that are concerned about the market. Some people tend to have knee-jerk reactions to things that are happening. For example, we are currently dealing with the Omicron variant of the Coronavirus. People think, "Should I go ahead and sell everything because the whole market is going to take a dive again?" It's an extreme example, but we saw it happen during the early stages of the pandemic in 2020, and we didn't have a knee-jerk reaction to that. So we have to utilize other tools such as economic indicators. We monitor various industry economics to look for cracks in the armor. Perhaps manufacturing or household goods start stalling. We can then make adjustments based on that information. With proper education, most of our clients understand that knee-jerk reactions are not beneficial. Sometimes we just have to talk them off the ledge a little.

Michael, what inspired you to get started in the financial services field?

Michael Nelan: That's a funny question. For me, it was a long time ago. I was in college, and I needed a job. Then, I saw an ad in the paper (before the internet), and they were hiring people for the securities business. At that time, everything was segmented. There were insurance people, stockbrokers, and in the case of this particular job ad, mutual fund people. This company sold mutual funds to teachers called 403Bs, or TSAs at the time. So they would help teachers put a savings program together with the mutual fund. It was funny because, back in the day, I didn't have a nice suit or a decent car. I was just a college kid trying to make it through life. I remember driving by and seeing all these people in line for the interviews, and they were all dressed in three-piece suits and holding briefcases. I was wearing khakis and a knit tie, and I thought to myself, "I can't compete with these guys." I turned my car around to head back home. I made it about two blocks before realizing these guys were no better than me. So I went back. They gave us a description of the job, and I thought it would be interesting to help people save for their future. I didn't know a thing about it, but it sounded great. I got the job, and it changed the trajectory of my entire life.

What should people look for when choosing a financial advisor?

Michael Nelan: It's really a gut thing, similar to choosing someone to do your taxes. Many people might think we are salesmen or just out to get a commission or a fee. But it's my job to educate people about the process and understand where they are financially. I honestly think it takes at least three to four conversations or visits with clients before moving forward on anything. If your check engine light comes on, the technician's first step is plugging your car into the computer to help determine what is going on. We do something similar with our analytical software. We have to see where a client's current portfolio is positioned and determine what level of risk they are willing to take before we make any recommendations. Sure, some stocks have done really well, and some people are looking for "home runs," but it doesn't work that way. We have to determine their level of risk, goals, and aspirations and then put together and monitor a program. People need to realize that it is a long-term process.

How can people find you, connect with you, and learn more?

Michael Nelan: Our phone number is 877-858-0906. You can also find us at www.fairoaksfinancialinc.com.

Securities and investment advisory services offered through Royal Alliance Associates, Inc. (RAA), member FINRA SIPC. RAA is separately owned and other entities and/or marketing names, products or services referenced here are independent of RAA. RAA does not provide tax or legal advice.

MICHAEL P. NELAN

President

Fair Oaks Financial, Inc.

In 1984, Michael began his financial services career helping teachers save for their retirement. To further increase his knowledge and service more clients, he joined Mutual of New York, a full-service insurance and financial services agency in Sacramento, California, where he prepared life & disability insurance proposals and financial plans for his clients. In 1987, Mr. Nelan accepted a position as a marketing representative for a California-based life insurance company where he assisted company agents with life and annuity products. To pursue his passion for helping clients and continue working with his own clients, Michael joined ORBA Financial Management Company in April 1997. He assisted approximately 250 financial advisors by preparing life insurance proposals, variable annuity product recommendations, detailed investment analysis, and financial planning support. In 2009, Michael started his own financial planning company, where he continues to serve his clients as a fully independent financial advisor.

In service to our country, Michael spent 12 years in the California Army National Guard and 27 years in the Nevada Air National Guard. He deployed overseas in support of Operation Iraqi Freedom and Operation Enduring Freedom. Having served a total of 39 years in the National Guard, Mr. Nelan retired on March 31, 2021, as the Aircraft Maintenance Group Superintendent.

EMAIL: mike@fairoaksfinancialinc.com

PHONE: 877-858-0906

WEBSITE: www.fairoaksfinancialinc.com

OTHER: www.nelanfinancial.com

BROCK BRENNEMAN

BROCK BRENNEMAN

Conversation with Brock Brenneman

Brock, you are a Managing Partner with Healthier Money. Tell us about your work and the people you help.

Brock Brenneman: Our firm is focused on reducing risk. We want to help people understand what they could potentially lose in a given month or year instead of just looking at what they might make. We believe that if we do a good job keeping people out of harm's way, especially with the unpredictability in the markets today, they should be able to accomplish their financial goals with more certainty. The kind of clients that we work with is twofold. I'm a little younger, so I enjoy working with people in the 30 to 50 range who are closer in age to me, usually still saving for retirement, and trying to plan and be proactive. Our Founder, Pat, is a little older, and he identifies really well with the 50 to 70 age range, who are either retired or very close to retirement age. At the end of the day, they just want to know they will be alright and have a plan that allows them to enjoy retirement comfortably.

What are the primary concerns of the younger clients?

Brock Brenneman: Don't think you have to be 30 to start financial planning. In fact, the earlier, the better. Many people my age tend to think, "Oh, I'll figure that out in the future." They just have way too much going on in life that they are trying to figure out and pay for. I start by looking at their cash flow based on income and expenses. If they have excess money each month, let's make sure we are efficient and allocate it to different places that suit their needs and goals. Even if you are never looking at it, you will have money going away toward future savings, and ideally, stuff that's earning interest well beyond what the bank might pay. So I really love working with those people because I know if they start now, even on a very small scale, they're going to be amazed at what they have in the future. It's so much easier when you are younger, and developing a plan and helping people realize that and take action makes me very excited about working in this business.

Are there common myths or misconceptions that prevent people from getting their finances in order?

Brock Brenneman: There is so much information out there, and everyone you talk to has a different opinion. You can talk to me and then speak to a friend or another professional, and we might have completely different views on the same topic. Neither of us is necessarily right or wrong, but I think sometimes all that information leads to overthinking, which leads to inaction.

Even if you're just putting money away into a basic savings account, in the worst-case scenario, you will at least have some savings built up, and you'll still be doing better than most people or better than you were before. Just try to get into the mindset of saving and putting money away. As you have more money down the road, we can start figuring out where to put it. Let's make sure it's as efficient as possible regarding potential losses or future tax implications. Most of the time, people just don't know what to do, so they don't start. You can start with as little as $10. Big companies online, such as Fidelity and Vanguard, have done a great job offering low-cost investments. You can open an account, and you don't need to pay a big-time advisor to help you when you're at that level. If you just set up an account and contribute $10 a month in things you identify with, you will be amazed at what you might have by the end of the year. I find that once people get started, they get really into it. They say, "Wow, I don't even miss that $10.

Maybe I could do $20 or even $100." And the next thing you know, they are really invested in their own plan.

Remember, you're not buying something or contributing $100 a month to your internet bill. You are putting it away to grow for the future, and depending on the account, sometimes it is accessible if you do get in a pinch. Today, especially with everything going on, you will feel so much better even if you just have a little money put away. With all the uncertainty out there, you will feel confident knowing you will be okay in case of an emergency. Ideally, just keep putting it away long-term. Nobody wants to work forever. If you want to retire at 50 or 60 or 70, that will only happen if you save and focus on your plan.

How has the recent pandemic impacted the financial services industry?

Brock Brenneman: Until Covid, we were on such a run of everything going up and everyone easily making money. I think the pandemic kind of shocked people a little bit. But frankly, it was so fast, and people came right back to normal that it's almost like they've forgotten about it already. One thing I have seen is people saying, "I'm a little worried if something like that happens again. I didn't really think about it before." I talked earlier about focusing on protection, and I've seen more people opening up to the concept of reducing their risk exposure and having a good plan instead of trying to do it all themselves. We believe two of the biggest things that hinder someone from having a successful retirement are the risk of increased taxes and market loss. If we can focus on solving for or limiting those risks, we feel our clients will be in a good spot throughout retirement and have more certainty in things working out for them.

Brock, what inspired you to get started in the financial services field?

Brock Brenneman: I had a job out of college that wasn't in this field. My co-workers and I were young, and we didn't really know what to do with our money, but we knew we wanted to be smart with it. One of my clients at that time was this company called Healthier Money, where I now work. I would always talk to them and be fascinated with their insight and ideas. I decided that I wanted to work for Healthier Money and help as many people as I could accomplish their financial goals. Now many of my old co-workers come to me with questions, and it has been rewarding to assist them in this field as well. I love that because I see their eyeballs light up when they realize they don't have to live paycheck to paycheck forever and can set up a really good plan for the future. That's how I got started. In the past few years, I have really grown in the business and with the company and am actively working with people one on one to implement their plans. Ideally, I get them to where they want to go with a lot more security and certainty.

What should people look for when choosing a financial advisor?

Brock Brenneman: I'll say two things. When I was young, I would Google "compound interest calculator." There are a couple of really good ones online. I would put in that I wanted to invest $500 each month for 20 years, and then it shows you a hypothetical dollar amount down the road based on what interest rate you put in. Then I would adjust the numbers slightly. Instead of 20 years of saving and growing, I would just put it at 18 or 19 years. That might not sound like a big difference, but you'll be amazed at how much less money you have in the future. If you take the time to really do that exercise, it should motivate you to get started now. By waiting one year, you might find that you have $30,000 less in your account down the road! You would probably get started if I paid you $30,000 right now. So let that be your motivation.

Secondly, when choosing a financial professional, I think it just all comes down to both of you being on the same page. I always tell people when we talk; it's just as much about me learning about you as you learning about me. You have to feel comfortable with me, and I have to feel that our long-term strategy fits what you're looking for. If you're telling me you want to get aggressive with crypto and stuff, that's fine, but that's not really what we do. We utilize more long-term, steady plans to focus on getting you where you want to be with some certainty. As soon as you and your advisor are not on the same page anymore, it's not going to work out. Everyone invests, saves, and plans differently. So choose someone you feel good about and trust.

How can people find you, connect with you, and learn more?

Brock Brenneman: Our firm, Healthier Money, is located in Arizona, but we have clients all over the country. My email is brock@healthiermoney.com. You can also give us a call at 602-789-3099. My direct extension is number two. We are active online, and you can find us on Facebook, YouTube, or LinkedIn as well. We would be happy to talk to anyone who has questions or wants to learn more about us, and we can make it happen no matter where you live these days.

BROCK BRENNEMAN

Managing Partner

Healthier Money

Originally from the Midwest, Brock moved to Arizona shortly after graduating from Indiana University. After working in business development for the Phoenix Suns, he joined the Healthier Money team in early 2019. Brock accepted the role at the firm, in large part because he saw how lost many of his coworkers were when it came to their own personal finances.

As Managing Partner of the firm, Brock is involved in all aspects of coordinating new business efforts, servicing current clients, developing new marketing initiatives, and staying up to date with the most current financial strategies. Brock prides himself on being someone his clients can trust – providing unbiased information that addresses their needs.

EMAIL: brock@healthiermoney.com

PHONE: 602-789-3099 x 2

WEBSITE: www.healthiermoney.com

ABOUT THE PUBLISHER

Mark Imperial is a Best-Selling Author, Syndicated Business Columnist, Syndicated Radio Host, and internationally recognized Stage, Screen, and Radio Host of numerous business shows spotlighting leading experts, entrepreneurs, and business celebrities.

His passion is to discover noteworthy business owners, professionals, experts, and leaders who do great work and share their stories and secrets to their success with the world on his syndicated radio program titled "Remarkable Radio."

Mark is also the media marketing strategist and voice for some of the world's most famous brands. You can hear his voice over the airwaves weekly on Chicago radio and worldwide on iHeart Radio.

Mark is a Karate black belt; teaches Muay Thai and Kickboxing; loves Thai food, House Music, and his favorite TV shows are infomercials.

Learn more:

www.MarkImperial.com
www.BooksGrowBusiness.com

Made in the USA
Monee, IL
04 November 2026

67376091R00066